Introduction to Augmented Reality (AR)

Augmented Reality (AR) is an interactive experience that superimposes computer-generated perceptual information onto the real world, enhancing one's current perception of reality. This technology seamlessly blends digital content with physical environments, creating a composite view that can engage multiple sensory modalities such as visual, auditory, haptic, somatosensory, and olfactory.

To understand AR fully, it is essential to delve into its origins. The concept of augmenting reality with digital information is not new, but its practical implementation began to take shape in the late 20th century. One of the earliest AR systems was developed in the early 1990s by Louis Rosenberg at the U.S. Air Force's Armstrong Laboratory. This pioneering system aimed to provide immersive mixed-reality experiences that could assist in complex tasks, such as those performed by pilots and engineers. By integrating digital overlays with the physical world, these early AR systems laid the groundwork for the future development of more sophisticated and user-friendly AR applications.

Milestones in AR Development:

ARToolKit (1999):

The development of ARToolKit in 1999 marked a significant milestone in the history of AR. ARToolKit is an open-source software library that enables the creation of AR applications by tracking the position and orientation of physical markers in real time. This technology allowed developers to overlay virtual objects onto the real world accurately, paving the way for a wide range of AR applications in education, gaming, and industrial design. For instance, a simple AR application built with ARToolKit might involve a user holding up a card with a specific pattern, which the software recognizes and uses to project a 3D model of a dinosaur on the screen, seamlessly blending it with the user's real-world environment.

Google Glass (2013):

In 2013, Google introduced Google Glass, a revolutionary AR device that brought augmented reality closer to mainstream consumers. Google Glass is a wearable headset that features a small display positioned near the user's eye, capable of projecting digital information into the user's field of vision. This innovation allowed users to access a wealth of information hands-free, such as navigation instructions, messages, and search results, directly in their line of sight. For example, a user navigating through a city could see turn-by-turn directions overlaid on the streets, making it easier to find their destination without looking down at a smartphone. Despite facing some privacy and usability concerns, Google Glass demonstrated the potential of wearable AR technology and inspired further advancements in the field.

Microsoft HoloLens (2015):

Microsoft HoloLens, launched in 2015, represents a significant leap forward in AR technology. Unlike previous AR devices, HoloLens is a standalone, mixed-reality headset that combines AR with spatial computing. It features advanced sensors, optics, and processing power to create holographic images that can interact with the physical environment. Users can manipulate these holograms using hand gestures, voice commands, and gaze tracking. For instance, an architect wearing HoloLens can visualize and interact with a 3D model of a building project directly on their desk, making design adjustments in real-time and collaborating with colleagues remotely. The ability to merge digital content with the real world in such an intuitive and immersive way has opened up new possibilities in fields such as healthcare, engineering, and entertainment.

Pokémon GO (2016):

The release of Pokémon GO in 2016 brought augmented reality to the forefront of popular culture. Developed by Niantic, this mobile game uses AR to place virtual Pokémon in the real world, allowing players to find, capture, and battle them using their smartphones. Pokémon GO's success demonstrated the widespread appeal and accessibility of AR technology, reaching millions of users worldwide and generating significant interest in AR applications. Players would walk around their neighborhoods, parks, and cities, discovering Pokémon that appeared as if they were actually present in their surroundings. This game not only highlighted the potential for AR in gaming but also showed how AR could encourage physical activity and social interaction.

The journey of AR from its early experimental systems to its current mainstream applications has been marked by significant milestones. Each development has contributed to the evolution of AR, making it more accessible, practical, and immersive. As technology continues to advance, the possibilities for augmented reality are virtually limitless, promising to transform how we interact with the world around us.

The Technological Breakthrough: Flexible, Transparent Displays

The evolution of flexible, transparent displays represents a significant leap in material science, driven by the development and refinement of various advanced materials. Among these, organic light-emitting diodes (OLEDs) stand out as a cornerstone technology. OLEDs are composed of organic compounds that emit light in response to an electric current. Their ability to produce bright, high-contrast images on thin, flexible substrates has made OLEDs a game-changer for display technology. Unlike traditional LEDs, OLEDs do not require a backlight, allowing for thinner and more energy-efficient screens. This innovation has paved the way for rollable, foldable, and even stretchable displays, which are increasingly finding applications in smartphones, wearables, and other portable devices.

Parallel to OLED advancements, innovations in graphene and other conductive polymers have further propelled the development of flexible, transparent displays. Graphene, a single layer of carbon atoms arranged in a hexagonal lattice, is renowned for its exceptional electrical conductivity, mechanical strength, and flexibility. When used in display technology, graphene can replace traditional, brittle conductors like indium tin oxide (ITO), enabling the creation of ultra-thin, flexible touchscreens. Conductive polymers, such as PEDOT:PSS, complement graphene's properties by offering additional flexibility and transparency, thus enhancing the overall performance and durability of next-generation displays.

3D Printing in AR:

The advent of 3D printing technology has revolutionized the rapid prototyping and production of complex components for augmented reality (AR) devices. 3D printing, or additive manufacturing, allows for the precise fabrication of intricate designs that would be challenging or impossible to achieve with traditional manufacturing methods. This capability is particularly beneficial for creating customized wearable AR devices tailored to individual users. For instance, an athlete might use a 3D-printed AR headset designed to fit their unique facial contours, ensuring maximum comfort and stability during intense physical activities.

In the realm of prosthetics, 3D printing has enabled the production of highly personalized, functional, and aesthetically pleasing prosthetic limbs. By integrating AR capabilities, these prosthetics can provide users with real-time feedback and enhanced control over their movements. Imagine a 3D-printed prosthetic hand equipped with AR sensors that guide the user in performing complex tasks, such as playing a musical instrument or typing on a keyboard, by overlaying visual cues and instructions onto their field of vision.

Advanced Polymers:

The role of advanced polymers in the development of flexible, transparent displays cannot be overstated. Polymers like polyvinyl alcohol (PVA) and polycarbonate are instrumental in creating displays that are not only flexible and durable but also lightweight and user-friendly. PVA, for instance, is known for its excellent film-forming properties, transparency, and flexibility. When used in display technology, PVA films can serve as substrates or encapsulation layers, protecting the delicate electronic components from environmental factors such as moisture and oxygen.

Polycarbonate, another critical polymer, offers high impact resistance and optical clarity, making it ideal for flexible display applications. Its durability ensures that the displays can withstand bending, folding, and other mechanical stresses without compromising performance. Moreover, the lightweight nature of polycarbonate contributes to the overall reduction in device weight, enhancing user comfort and portability. A smartphone with a flexible, polycarbonate-based display, for example, can be rolled up and easily carried in a pocket or small bag, providing unprecedented convenience and versatility.

Impact on Device Weight, Flexibility, and User Comfort:

The integration of flexible, transparent displays into electronic devices has profound implications for their weight, flexibility, and user comfort. Traditional glass-based displays are rigid and often heavy, limiting their applications and making them prone to damage from impacts and drops. In contrast, flexible displays made from advanced materials like OLEDs, graphene, and specialized polymers are significantly lighter and more resilient. This reduction in weight is particularly advantageous for wearable devices, such as AR headsets and smartwatches, which must be comfortable to wear for extended periods.

Furthermore, the inherent flexibility of these displays allows for new form factors and design possibilities. Devices can now be designed to bend, fold, or even stretch, offering enhanced durability and user interaction. For example, a foldable smartphone can transition from a compact device to a larger tablet-like display, providing users with a versatile tool for both communication and media consumption. The flexibility also enhances the user experience by reducing the risk of screen damage and making the devices more ergonomic.

The technological breakthroughs in flexible, transparent displays are the result of advancements in material science, 3D printing, and advanced polymers. These innovations have collectively transformed the landscape of electronic devices, making them more adaptable, durable, and user-friendly. As research and development in these areas continue to progress, we can expect even more revolutionary applications and improvements in the devices we use every day.

Wearable Devices and the Metaverse:

The evolution of wearable technology has been a remarkable journey, marked by significant advancements that have transformed early, bulky headsets into sleek, integrated glasses. Initially, wearable devices focused primarily on providing basic augmented reality (AR) experiences through head-mounted displays. These early headsets were often cumbersome and limited in functionality, primarily used for industrial and military applications where their size and weight were less of an issue.

As technology progressed, the miniaturization of components and improvements in display and battery technologies led to the development of more sophisticated and user-friendly wearable devices. A prime example of this evolution is the Vuzix Blade, a pair of smart glasses that resemble traditional eyewear but are equipped with AR capabilities. The Vuzix Blade allows users to access digital information such as notifications, navigation, and real-time translations directly in their field of vision, all while maintaining a lightweight and comfortable design.

Another notable example is the Magic Leap One, a mixed-reality headset that blends digital content with the real world in an immersive and interactive manner. Unlike its predecessors, the Magic Leap One offers a more natural and intuitive user experience by integrating advanced sensors, spatial audio, and a high-resolution display. This device enables users to interact with holograms and digital objects as if they were part of the physical environment, opening up new possibilities for gaming, education, and professional applications.

The Metaverse:

The concept of the Metaverse represents the next frontier in digital interaction, envisioning a collective virtual shared space where virtually enhanced physical reality converges with physically persistent virtual spaces. The Metaverse is more than just a virtual world; it is an interconnected ecosystem of digital environments where users can interact, socialize, and create in ways that transcend the limitations of the physical world.

Augmented reality plays a crucial role in bringing the Metaverse to life by providing the tools and technologies needed to create immersive and interconnected virtual worlds. AR enhances the user's perception of reality by overlaying digital content onto the physical environment, creating a seamless blend of the real and virtual. This capability is essential for developing the immersive experiences that define the Metaverse, allowing users to navigate and interact with virtual spaces as naturally as they do in the real world.

Key players in the development of the Metaverse include major technology companies and innovative startups, each contributing to the growth and evolution of this digital frontier. One of the most prominent examples is Facebook's Horizon, a social VR platform that allows users to create and explore virtual worlds, socialize with others, and participate in a wide range of activities. Horizon aims to create a shared virtual space where people can connect and collaborate in ways that are not possible in the physical world.

Decentraland is another key player in the Metaverse, offering a decentralized virtual world built on blockchain technology. In Decentraland, users can purchase, develop, and trade virtual land, creating their own unique digital experiences and economies. This platform highlights the potential of the Metaverse to not only provide entertainment and social interaction but also to create new opportunities for economic activity and digital entrepreneurship.

The synergy between wearable technology and the Metaverse is driving the next wave of digital innovation. The evolution of sleek, integrated wearable devices like the Vuzix Blade and Magic Leap One, combined with the expansive vision of interconnected virtual spaces, is transforming how we interact with both the digital and physical worlds. As AR continues to advance, it will play an increasingly vital role in shaping the Metaverse, offering immersive, interactive experiences that redefine the boundaries of reality.

AR in Education

Augmented Reality (AR) is revolutionizing the educational landscape by providing dynamic, interactive learning experiences that engage students in unprecedented ways. AR transforms traditional textbooks into interactive platforms where students can visualize and interact with 3D models, bringing abstract concepts to life. For example, an AR-enabled biology textbook might allow students to explore a 3D model of the human heart, observing its structure and functions from various angles and interacting with it to see how blood flows through its chambers. This hands-on approach facilitates deeper understanding and retention of complex subjects.

One notable application of AR in education is Google Expeditions, which offers virtual field trips that transport students to distant places and historical periods without leaving the classroom. Through AR, students can explore the Great Wall of China, dive into the depths of the ocean, or walk through ancient Rome.

These immersive experiences not only make learning more engaging but also broaden students' perspectives, enhancing their appreciation of different cultures and environments.

AR Flashcards are another innovative tool that uses AR to make learning more interactive and fun for younger students. By pointing a device's camera at special flashcards, students can see animated 3D models that correspond to the content on the cards. For instance, a flashcard with the letter "A" might display a 3D apple, which students can rotate and view from different angles. This visual and interactive approach helps children associate letters with objects, improving their literacy skills in an engaging manner.

Benefits:

The benefits of AR in education are manifold, with enhanced engagement being one of the most significant. Interactive content captivates students' attention and makes learning more enjoyable, leading to increased motivation and participation. For example, a history lesson on ancient Egypt becomes much more exciting when students can virtually explore a 3D model of a pyramid, walk through its chambers, and uncover hidden artifacts. This level of engagement encourages active learning, where students are more involved and curious about the subject matter.

Improved comprehension is another crucial benefit of AR in education. Visualization of complex concepts through 3D models and interactive simulations aids in better understanding. For instance, in a physics class, students can use AR to visualize and manipulate forces and vectors in real time, helping them grasp the principles of motion and mechanics more effectively than traditional diagrams and lectures alone. The ability to see and interact with concepts in a tangible way bridges the gap between theoretical knowledge and practical application, fostering a deeper comprehension of the subject.

Challenges:

Despite its many advantages, the integration of AR in education is not without challenges. One significant barrier is the cost of AR technology. High-quality AR devices and software can be expensive, making it difficult for some schools, particularly those in underfunded areas, to adopt this technology. Schools need to invest in AR-compatible devices such as tablets or smartphones, as well as the necessary software and applications. These costs can add up quickly, creating financial hurdles for widespread implementation.

Another challenge is the need for teacher training and curriculum integration. Teachers must be proficient in using AR technology to effectively incorporate it into their lessons. This requires comprehensive training programs to familiarize educators with AR tools and applications, as well as ongoing support to help them integrate AR into their existing curricula. Additionally, developing and aligning AR content with educational standards and learning objectives can be time-consuming and complex. Educators need to ensure that AR activities are not just engaging but also intellectually sound and aligned with the curriculum.

AR has the potential to transform education by making learning more interactive, engaging, and comprehensible. However, addressing the challenges of cost and the need for teacher training and curriculum integration is essential for its successful implementation. As technology continues to evolve and become more accessible, the future of AR in education looks promising, offering exciting possibilities for enriching the learning experiences of students worldwide.

AR in Healthcare

Augmented Reality (AR) is revolutionizing healthcare, particularly in the realm of medical training. AR provides realistic simulations that are invaluable for surgical training, allowing medical students and professionals to practice and refine their skills in a risk-free environment. For instance, AR-based anatomy apps enable users to explore detailed 3D models of human anatomy. These apps provide an interactive way to study the body's structures, offering a level of detail and engagement that traditional textbooks cannot match. By overlaying digital information onto a physical model or a real patient's body, these tools enhance the learning experience and improve the understanding of complex anatomical relationships.

One practical application of AR in medical training is AccuVein, a device that projects a map of veins onto the skin, making it easier for healthcare professionals to locate veins for intravenous (IV) insertions. This technology not only reduces the discomfort and anxiety for patients but also increases the success rate of first-attempt insertions. AccuVein exemplifies how AR can combine real-world practice with digital augmentation to enhance medical training and patient care.

Benefits:

The benefits of AR in healthcare extend beyond training into actual clinical practice. One of the primary advantages is enhanced precision in surgical procedures. AR systems can provide surgeons with detailed, real-time visualizations of a patient's anatomy during operations. For example, during a complex brain surgery, AR can overlay critical structures such as blood vessels and tumors onto the surgeon's field of view, allowing for more precise navigation and reducing the risk of damaging vital tissues. This real-time guidance can significantly improve surgical outcomes and reduce the likelihood of complications.

Another key benefit is the real-time data overlay for diagnostics. AR can superimpose diagnostic information, such as MRI or CT scan results, directly onto a patient's body during examinations. This capability enables doctors to see inside the patient without making incisions, providing a clearer understanding of underlying conditions. For instance, an AR system might project the location of a tumor onto a patient's body during a physical examination, helping the doctor assess the tumor's size and position more accurately. This immediate access to critical data can enhance the accuracy of diagnoses and the effectiveness of treatment plans.

Challenges:

Despite its transformative potential, the integration of AR in healthcare faces several challenges. One significant hurdle is obtaining regulatory approvals. Healthcare technologies must undergo rigorous testing and validation to ensure they meet safety and efficacy standards set by regulatory bodies such as the Food and Drug Administration (FDA) in the United States. The approval process can be lengthy and complex, requiring substantial evidence from clinical trials and studies. This regulatory scrutiny is essential to protect patient safety, but it can also slow the adoption of innovative AR technologies in the medical field.

Ensuring patient data privacy and security is another critical challenge. AR systems often rely on patient data to function effectively, raising concerns about how this sensitive information is stored, accessed, and protected. Healthcare providers must implement robust cybersecurity measures to prevent data breaches and unauthorized access. Additionally, they must comply with stringent data protection regulations, such as the Health Insurance Portability and Accountability Act (HIPAA) in the United States, which governs the handling of patient information. Balancing the benefits of AR with the need to safeguard patient privacy requires ongoing vigilance and adherence to best practices in data security.

AR is poised to make a significant impact on healthcare by enhancing medical training, improving surgical precision, and providing real-time diagnostic information. However, the successful implementation of AR technologies hinges on overcoming regulatory challenges and ensuring the privacy and security of patient data. As these obstacles are addressed, AR has the potential to transform healthcare delivery, offering safer, more efficient, and more effective medical care.

The Future of Augmented Reality

The future of Augmented Reality (AR) promises to revolutionize various industries, offering innovative applications that enhance user experiences in retail, entertainment, and real estate.

Retail: Virtual Try-Ons and Enhanced Shopping Experiences

In retail, AR is set to transform how consumers shop by enabling virtual try-ons and providing enhanced shopping experiences. Virtual try-ons allow customers to see how clothes, accessories, or even makeup look on them without physically wearing the items. For instance, companies like IKEA and Sephora have developed AR apps that let users visualize furniture in their homes or test different makeup looks using their smartphones. This technology not only makes shopping more convenient but also reduces the likelihood of returns, as customers can make more informed purchasing decisions. Imagine walking into a store, trying on multiple outfits virtually using an AR mirror, and instantly seeing how they fit and look from all angles without stepping into a fitting room.

Entertainment: Immersive Gaming and Live Events

The entertainment industry is also poised to benefit significantly from AR. Immersive gaming experiences are already becoming a reality, with games like Pokémon GO demonstrating the potential for AR to blend digital gameplay with the real world. Future AR games will likely offer even more interactive and engaging experiences, allowing players to interact with virtual characters and environments in their actual surroundings. Beyond gaming, AR can enhance live events such as concerts and sports matches by overlaying real-time statistics, player information, and other interactive elements onto the viewer's field of vision. Picture attending a football game and seeing player stats and game analytics projected onto the field through AR glasses, enriching the live event experience.

Real Estate: Virtual Property Tours

In real estate, AR is transforming how properties are showcased and sold. Virtual property tours allow potential buyers to explore homes and commercial spaces remotely, providing a detailed and immersive experience without the need for physical visits. Real estate agents can use AR to overlay information about the property, such as room dimensions, renovation possibilities, and neighborhood amenities, directly onto the real-world view of the property. This technology is particularly valuable in a global market, where buyers might be considering properties in different cities or countries. For example, a prospective buyer in New York could virtually tour a beachfront property in Miami, examining every detail as if they were there in person.

Trends:

Several key trends are shaping the future of AR, with significant advancements expected in the integration of artificial intelligence (AI) and the development of AR glasses and contact lenses.

Integration with AI for Smarter AR Experiences

The integration of AI with AR is set to create smarter, more intuitive AR experiences. AI can enhance AR applications by providing context-aware interactions and real-time data processing. For example, AI algorithms can analyze a user's environment and behavior to deliver personalized AR content. In a retail setting, an AI-powered AR app could suggest clothing items based on the user's style preferences and previous purchases. Additionally, AI can improve object recognition and tracking, making AR experiences more seamless and responsive. Imagine an AR navigation app that not only guides you to your destination but also provides real-time information about landmarks, traffic conditions, and nearby amenities based on your interests and preferences.

Growth in AR Glasses and Contact Lenses:

Another significant trend is the growth in AR glasses and contact lenses. These devices are evolving rapidly, becoming more compact, comfortable, and capable. AR glasses, such as the Vuzix Blade and Magic Leap One, are already available, offering hands-free access to digital information and interactive experiences. Future iterations of AR glasses are expected to be even more lightweight and stylish, blending seamlessly with everyday eyewear. Additionally, research is underway to develop AR contact lenses that can project digital content directly onto the user's eyes. These lenses would provide a truly immersive and unobtrusive AR experience, revolutionizing how we interact with digital information. Imagine reading text messages, getting navigation directions, or accessing vital health data directly through your contact lenses without needing a smartphone or glasses.

The future of AR is bright, with transformative applications in retail, entertainment, and real estate. As AR technology continues to advance, driven by trends such as AI integration and the development of AR glasses and contact lenses, we can expect more immersive, personalized, and convenient experiences that enhance various aspects of our daily lives. The continued innovation in AR promises to blur the lines between the digital and physical worlds, creating a new reality where the possibilities are virtually limitless.

Summary

The advancements in flexible, transparent displays have had a profound impact on the development and application of augmented reality (AR) technology. These displays, made possible by breakthroughs in material science and innovations such as OLEDs and graphene, have enabled the creation of lightweight, durable, and versatile devices. Their integration into wearable technology has transformed AR from a concept into a practical tool that enhances our daily lives.

In education, AR is revolutionizing learning by providing interactive textbooks, 3D models, and virtual field trips. These tools engage students in ways traditional methods cannot, making learning more immersive and effective. Similarly, in healthcare, AR is transforming medical training and practice. Realistic simulations for surgical training, real-time data overlays during procedures, and enhanced diagnostic capabilities are just a few examples of how AR is improving precision, efficiency, and outcomes in the medical field.

Final Thoughts:

As we look towards the future, it is clear that AR will continue to play an increasingly significant role in various aspects of our lives. The potential for AR to transform industries such as retail, entertainment, and real estate is immense, offering new ways to interact with digital content and the physical world.

To fully harness the benefits of AR, it is crucial to stay informed about the latest advancements and trends. The integration of AI with AR, the development of AR glasses and contact lenses, and the continuous improvement in display technology are just some areas to watch. By staying updated, individuals and businesses can be better prepared to adopt and leverage AR technology as it evolves.

In envisioning an AR-integrated future, we see a world where the lines between the digital and physical realms are increasingly blurred. AR will enable us to access information effortlessly, interact with virtual environments seamlessly, and enhance our understanding and capabilities in ways previously unimaginable. This vision of the future, driven by continuous innovation and adoption of AR, promises a more connected, efficient, and enriched world.

As we embrace these advancements, the transformative potential of AR will become even more apparent, reshaping our experiences, industries, and interactions in profound and exciting ways.

www.ingramcontent.com/pod-product-compliance
Lightning Source LLC
Chambersburg PA
CBHW070905070326
40690CB00009B/2010